INTERNATIONAL COMBAT AIKI-JUJUTSU FEDERATION

AIKI-JUJUTSU MANUAL

Darel E. Chase – 8th Dan, Kyoshi
Kaicho

ICAJF Aiki-jujutsu Manual

By: Darel E. Chase, Kyoshi

ISBN: 978-0-557-71538-1

First Edition

Disclaimer:

This book contains the full catalogue of ICAJF Aiki-jujutsu, containing the required techniques of the ICAJF Aiki-jujutsu system. The techniques and philosophies contained herein are potentially dangerous and may cause permanent injury or death. It is advised that great caution be applied in administering the techniques, and that these techniques are practiced under the supervision of a qualified Instructor of ICAJF Aiki-jujutsu.

International Combat Aiki-jujutsu Federation, Darel E. Chase, its instructors, agents and or volunteers are not responsible for any loss or damage that may occur as a result of practicing and/or applying the techniques of ICAJF Aiki-jujutsu.

Printed in the USA

Table of Contents

Catalogue of Required Techniques

Please note that the International Combat Aiki-jujutsu Federation teaches the traditional method of Aiki Jujutsu. Therefore, the following list of techniques is presented as an overall guide, not a specific or chronological listing of techniques for advancement. Students are encouraged to seek out the basics and master them before moving on to higher or more advanced techniques.

Ukemi Waza: (Safety/Falling Techniques)

- **Mae Ukemi** – Front/Forward Break Fall
- **Ushiro Ukemi** – Back/Rearward Break Fall
- **Yoko Ukemi** – Side Break Fall (Migi/Right & Hidari/Left)
- **Zenpo Kaiten Ukemi** – Forward Roll Break Fall
- **Ushiro Kaiten Ukemi** – Backward Roll Break Fall
- **Yoko Mawashi Ukemi** – Side Turning Break Fall
- **Zenpo Sansui Ukemi** – Forward Diving Roll Break Fall
- **Chgaeri Ukemi** – Somersault Break Fall

Geri Waza: (Kicking Techniques)

- **Mae Geri** – Front Kick (Kekomi/Snapping & Keage/Thrusting)
- **Yoko Geri** – Side Kick (Kekomi & Keage)
- **Mawashi Geri** – Roundhouse Kick
- **Mikazuki Geri** – Crescent Kick (Uchi/Inside & Soto/Outside)
- **Kage Geri** – Hook Kick
- **Ushiro Geri** – Back Kick
- **Mae Tobi Geri** – Jumping Front Kick
- **Mawashi Tobi Geri** – Jumping Roundhouse Kick
- **Yoko Tobi Geri** – Jumping Side Kick

Yawara: (Basic Hand Techniques)

- **Kakate Hazushi Ichi** – Outside Wrist Release
- **Kakate Hazushi Ni** – Inside Wrist Release
- **Morote Hazushi** – Two-on-one Wrist Release
- **Ryote Hazushi** – Double Wrist Grab Release
- **Momiji Hazushi** – Front Choke Hold Release
- **Ryoeri Hazushi** – Double Lapel Grab Release
- **Yubi Tori Hazushi** – Release from Four Finger Grip
- **Yubi Tori** – Handhold on Sensitive Third Finger
- **Moro Yubi** – Four Finger Come-Along

Imon Tori – Defense against Chest Push
Ryoeri Tori – Double Lapel Torture Hold
Akushu Kote Tori – Handshake into Wristlock
Akushu Ude Tori – Straight Armbar from Handshake

__Atemi Waza__: (Striking/Vital Area Techniques)
Kami no Ke – Hair Grab
Gansei – Eye Rake
Hamaoshi – Nose Press
Nodo Hikui – Lower Throat
Kyosen – Solar Plexus
Yoko Tsukiage – Side Stab
Jinzo – Kidney or Hips
Kinsho – Groin Stab
Momo Tsunoru – Shark Bite
Kori – Foot
Mimi Oshi – Ear Press
Seidon – Jaw or Cheek
Dokko – Neck
Kakon – Ear or Lip Twist
Kyoka – Pectoral Muscle or Armpit
Hijizuma – Ulna Nerve
Kodenko – Lower Back
Kusamaki – Calf
Kokei – Shin
Uchikurobushi – Ankle
Bisen – Nose
Mimi Tsuki – Ear Clap
Gansai – Eye Gouge
Koka – Neck or Throat
Kensen – High Shoulder or Collarbone
Koraku – Hand or Biceps
Getsui – Floating Ribs
Tsuki Mata – Groin Pull
Hiza – Knee (kick)
Kori – Foot Stomp
Komekani – Temple
Mikazaki – Jaw
Hokkyoku – Base of Skull
Ganka – Heart
Tanden – Lower Stomach
Katsusatsu – Spine

Bitei – Tailbone
Fukuto – Thigh
Kokei – Shin
Kusamaki – Calf Muscle

Atemi Waza is an important part of Aiki Jujutsu training. In the application of such techniques, the student/practitioner is required to utilize precision and control in demonstrating such techniques.
Each separate technique is designed to have a specific result on a particular part of the body. It is recommended that the student/practitioner study to discover the potency of the technique through the meridian/nerve path and/or pressure point attacked.

__Shime no Kata__: (Constriction & Strangulation)

Hadaka Shime Ichi – Front Choke or Neck Breaker
Hadaka Shime Ni – Rear Arm Choke
Namijuji Shime – Choke with Fingers Inside
Gyakujuji Shime – Choke with Thumbs Inside
Osaegami Shime – Hair and Chin Neck Breaker
Eri Gatame – Throw and Apply Headlock Arm Inside
Kata Gatame – Throw and Apply Headlock Arm Outside
Ashi Nada Shime – Japanese Legbar
Tsukikomi Shime – Thrusting Knuckle Choke
Sankaku Gatame – Figure Four Leg Strangle
Dakikubi Shime – Headlock Throw and Neck-hold

Shime Waza are strangulation and constriction techniques, which are utilized to prevent the Uke's blood flow and/or to cut off their breathing.
Extreme control in the Dojo setting is expected. Serious damage may result in the application and/or demonstration of these techniques.

__Nage no Kata__: (Forms of Throwing)

Kakato Otoshi – Heel to Heel Trip
Osoto Gari – Pendulum Sweep
Deashi Harai – Lower Foot Sweep
Ogoshi – Major Hip Throw
Tsurikomi Goshi – Lift and Pull Hip Throw
Ippon Seoi Nage – One Arm Shoulder Throw
Dakikubi Goshi – Headlock Hip Throw
Sode Tsurikomi Goshi – Lift and Pull Sleeve Hip Throw
Soto Gama – Outside Sickle
Uchi Gama – Inside Sickle
Tai Otoshi – Body Drop
Tani Otoshi – Valley Drop
Seoi Nage – Shoulder Throw

Seoi Otoshi – Shoulder Drop
Makikomi – Winding Art/Snake Throw
Wazakomi – Winding Arm Throw
Tome Nage – Stomach Throw
Kubi Nage – Neck Throw
Kubi Otoshi – Neck Drop
Sekui Nage – Scooping Throw
Kesa Nage – Scarf Throw
Yama Arashi – Mountain Storm
Uki Otoshi – Floating Throw
Okuri Harai – Side Stepping Throw
Kote Gaeshi – Wrist Throw
Hane Goshi – Bent Knee Hip Throw
Harai Goshi – Loin to Ankle Sweep
Shiho Nage – Four Corner Throw

Nage Waza (Throwing Techniques) are applied for the purpose of taking an attacker down and finishing him off. International Combat Aiki-jujutsu Federation utilizes both Judo and traditional Aiki-jujutsu type throwing techniques. Extreme caution is to be observed and proper Ukemi is to be exercised at all times. Sever and permanent damage may occur if throws and/or Ukemi is not properly applied.

Aiki-jujutsu utilizes ***Aiki***, which is internal energy/life-force. There are throwing techniques at higher levels, which utilize Ki as well as momentum and the force of the attackers strength and power against themselves.
Again, extreme caution and control is to be applied at all times.

Kyusho no Kata: (Pressure Points/Vital Areas)

Cheek Bone
Under Eye
Jugular Vein
Corrodid Artery
Web of Hand (between Thumb and Forefinger)
Wrist Point 1
Wrist Point 2
Forearm Point 1
Forearm Point 2
Forearm Point 3
Elbow Point 1
Elbow Point 2
Elbow Point 3
Bicep Point 1

Bicep Point 2
Pectoral Muscle Point 1
Pectoral muscle point 2
Armpit
Sternum
Bridge of Nose
Septum
Upper Lip
Lower Lip
Behind Ear
Trapizius Muscle
Collarbone
Trachea
Solar Plexus
Tanden
Groin Point 1
Groin Point 2
Groin Point 3
Hamstrings
Quadriceps
Above Knee
Shin
Calf Muscle
Behind Knee

Please note that these points are utilized for finishing moves and/or controlling techniques. These pressure points are dangerous and should be attacked with precision and skill.

Absolutely no student who does not have the permission of the Senior Shihan should attempt to utilize these pressure points and controlling techniques.

Pressure Point techniques may cause sever and permanent damage. It is a known fact that techniques delivered to pressure points can cause unconsciousness, paralysis and may also cause brain damage.

Caution is to be exercised at all times in the demonstration, practice and utilization of these techniques.

Goshin no Kata: (Self-Defense Techniques)

1. Defense from Straight Punch
2. Defense from Front Kick
3. Defense from Side Kick
4. Defense from Roundhouse Kick
5. Defense from Overhead Attack
6. Defense from Front Chokehold
7. Defense from Rear Chokehold
8. Defense from Side Headlock
9. Defense from Front Headlock
10. Defense from Overhead Club Attack
11. Defense from Swinging Club Attack
12. Defense from Choking Club Attack
13. Defense from Stabbing Club Attack
14. Defense from Stabbing Knife Attack
15. Defense from Swinging Knife Attack
16. Defense from Knife at Throat Attack
17. Defense from Knife at Throat Rear Attack
18. Defense from Gun at Back Attack
19. Defense from Gun at Side Attack
20. Defense from Gun at Head Attack
21. Defense from Gun at Stomach Attack
22. Disarming of Long Sword #1
23. Disarming of Long Sword #2
24. Disarming of Long Sword #3
25. Disarming of Short Sword #1
26. Disarming of Short Sword #2
27. Disarming of Short Sword #3
28. Hanbo Disarming Techniques #1 - #5
29. Bo Disarming Techniques #1 - #5
30. Cane Techniques #1 - #10

Please note that the Goshin (Self-Defense) techniques provided in this list are only meant to serve as a general guideline. All techniques listed may be combined with other techniques and be useful for self-defense. It should be noted that Aiki-jujutsu self-defense techniques (in the traditional sense) do not cover gun-disarming techniques. However, International Combat Aiki-jujutsu Federation believes in preparation for any and all attacks against one's- self, including modern weaponry. Most of the Goshin Waza are traditional techniques of Aiki-jujutsu. It should be studied and applied both in traditional and modern terms for the benefit of self-protection.

Seiza no Kata: (Traditional Seated Defense)

Sentou-ryu Aikikai practices traditional Aiki-jujutsu. There are approximately ***25*** seated defenses, which the student/practitioner must learn. For the sake of listing said techniques, the Seiza no Kata curriculum has been listed in numerical order.

1. Seiza Kata Ichi
2. Seiza Kata Ni
3. Seiza Kata San
4. Seiza Kata Shi
5. Seiza Kata Go
6. Seiza Kata Roku
7. Seiza Kata Shichi
8. Seiza Kata Hachi
9. Seiza Kata Ku
10. Seiza Kata Ju
11. Seiza Kata Ju-Ichi
12. Seiza Kata Ju-Ni
13. Seiza Kata Ju-San
14. Seiza Kata Ju-Shi
15. Seiza Kata Ju-Go
16. Seiza Kata Ju-Roku
17. Seiza Kata Ju-Shichi
18. Seiza Kata Ju-Hachi
19. Seiza Kata Ju-Ku
20. Seiza Kata Ni-Ju
21. Seiza Kata Ni-Ju-Ichi
22. Seiza Kata Ni-Ju-Ni
23. Seiza Kata Ni-Ju-San
24. Seiza Kata Ni-Ju-Shi
25. Seiza Kata Ni-Ju-Go

Seiza Kata are a traditional and very important part of Aiki-jujutsu. Each Kata runs through a series of techniques, ranging from unarmed and armed attacks from various positions.

At the upper level of these Kata, the principles of authentic Aiki are applied. These Kata also range from single to multiple attacker scenarios.

Control and precision of technique should be mastered, as these traditional seated defenses are applied. Student/practitioners are encouraged to expand on the traditional application to "create" applications for various scenarios for today's environments. However, for examination/certification purposes, each Kata is to be demonstrated in its traditional application.

Proper Uniform

Members of the Sentou-ryu Aikikai are to wear traditional *white* Gi and proper Obi. Only Instructors holding the rank of Hachidan or above, who are certified Instructors of ICAJF may adorn Black Gis.

The Kamon (emblem) of the International Combat Aiki-jujutsu Federation is to be worn over the right breast of the Gi jacket. No other patches, emblems or insignia may be worn.

Hakama are to be worn in regular teaching session by the Senior Yudansha only. During ranking ceremonies all Yudansha are to wear Hakama. Obi (belts) are not to be worn with the Hakama at all (this is very inappropriate).

Black Belt (Yudansha) are to wear Obi 2" inches wide and embroidered in red only, unless the Black Belt has obtained the specific teaching certification of Renshi or above – in which case, the Black Belt is permitted to darn gold embroidery. Only certified Renshi are to wear the Red/White and Black Belt. Only those holding the title and certification of Shihan are to wear the Red and White panel belt.

There shall be no stray threads on any uniform. The Gi is to be neat (clean and white or clean and black – depending upon rank).

Finger and toenails are to be trimmed at all times (this is a safety precaution). All members must practice personal hygiene (cleanliness) at all times.

Use of proper titles and adherence to etiquette are a must. Therefore, all student/practitioners are to address Black Belts in the proper manner. If in the event that the specific title of the Black Belt is unknown, the student/practitioner is to address the Black Belt as Sir or Ma'am.

Proper Titles

NOTE:

Use the proper titles and terms when addressing Black Belts. The proper titles are as follows:

Shidoshi (Instructor) – A Black Belt from Shodan to Sandan not holding Menkyo status.

Sensei (Teacher) – A Black Belt from Sandan or higher.

Renshi (Polished Instructor) – A Black Belt holding the rank of Godan or higher and holds the certification of ***Renshi***.

Shihan (Chief/Master Instructor) – A Black Belt holding the rank of Rokudan or higher and holds the certification of ***Shihan***.

Kyoshi (Chief/Master Instructor) – A Black Belt holding the rank of Shichidan or higher and holds the certification of ***Kyoshi***.

Hanshi (Chief/Master Instructor) – A Black Belt holding the rank of Hachidan or higher and holds the certification of ***Hanshi***.

Dai Shihan (Senior Master Instructor) – A Black Belt holding the rank of Hachidan or higher and has acquired the status of ***Menkyo Kaiden***.

Soke (Head of Family) – A Black Belt holding the rank of Godan or higher who has completed all requirements of all levels of Menkyo certification and has been bestowed with inheritorship of the ryu-ha, Kai or system.

Kaiso (Originator/Founder of the Family): this title/designation belongs rightfully only to the Founder and originator of an Aiki-budo system. He is to be addressed as ***Kaiso***.

JAPANESE TERMINOLOGY FOR MARTIAL ARTS

Basic Commands

Shomen ni rei - *sho-men nee ray* Bow to the "high" or shrine side of the Dojo
Sensei ni rei - *sen-say nee ray* Bow to the Teacher
Shihan ni rei - *she-hon nee ray* Bow to the Master
Soke ni rei - *so-kay nee ray* Bow to the Soke
Yudansha ni rei - *you-dahn-shah nee ray* Bow to the Black Belts
Sempai ni rei - *sem-pie nee ray* Bow to the Senior Student
Hajime - *hah-jih-may* Begin/Start
Yame - *yah-may* Stop/Hault
Mate - *mah-tay* Wait/Pause

Basic Terminology

Atemi - *ah-tem-me* Striking to vital points
Tsuki - *zooh-kee* Punching
Geri - *gerh-ee* Kicking
Nage - *nah-geh* Throwing
Barai - *bar-iee* Sweeping
Uke - *ooh-kay* Blocking; also the person who initiates the attack and receives the technique
Tori - *toe-ree* the person who receives the attack and initiates the technique
Jujutsu - *jew-jhut-soo* a compound word consisting of two elements "Ju" meaning gentle or yielding and "Jutsu" meaning art; an unarmed form of Martial Art utilizing blocking, kicking, punching, striking, throwing, grappling, joint-locking and strangulation/constriction techniques. Literally meaning "Gentle Art" or "Soft Art"; a form of Martial Arts founded in Japan by Samurai Warriors for the purpose of unarmed combat approximately 3000 years ago
Aiki - *iee-kee* the philosophy, art and application of ones internal energy or life essence; Literally meaning "Harmony of Spirit" also harmony of energy and nature, a blending of energy
Ryu - *ree-ooh* a method, philosophy or school of thought and/or application

Sentou – *sen-toh* combat, battle

Karate - *kah-rah-tay* a compound word consisting of two elements "Kara" meaning empty or open and "Te" meaning hand; a form of Martial Arts founded in Japan approximately 300 - 400 years ago consisting of kicking, punching, blocking and kata (forms)

Kiai - *kee-iee* spirit yell, also spirit wind; the shout expelled when delivering a strike or technique

Kata - *kah-tah* prearranged sequence of movement; a form; a sequence of movements emulating combatant techniques

Dan - *dohn* a Black Belt grade rank ranging from 1st - 10th degree

Yudansha - *yoo-dohn-shah* members holding Black Belt ranks (collectively)

Mudansha - *moo-dohn-shah* members holding Kyu grade/Color Belt ranks (collectively)

Kyu - *keew* a student grade rank ranging from 10th - 1st level

Menkyo - *mhen-kee-oh* a certificate of teaching authority ranging from ***Shoden*** (basic), ***Chuden*** (intermediate), ***Okuden*** (advanced) level transmission as well as "***Menkyo Kaiden***," which is a teaching certificate of full proficiency in the art

Dojo - *doh-joh* a hall used for training; Literally, "the place of the way"

Migi - *mih-ghee* to the right or right side

Hidari - *hih-dar-ee* to the left or left side

Ushiro - *oo-shih-roh* back-side or backward

Jodan - *joh-dohn* high or upper level

Chudan - *chew-dohn* middle or mid range level

Gedan - *ghee-dohn* low or low range level

Kai - *khiee* an association or organization

Goshin - *goh-shin* self-defense and/or personal protection

Waza - *wah-zah* technique or application of technique

Kansetsu - *khan-set-soo* joint locking

Othoshi - *oh-toe-she* a form of throwing or dropping

Nage – *nah-geh* a form of throwing; throwing techniques (i.e. Nage Waza)

Gari - *ghar-rhee* a form of sweeping

Taisabaki - *tie-sah-bah-kee* body rotation, pivoting and movement

Shime - *shih-meh* strangulation and constriction
Gatame - *gah-tah-meh* grappling
Kyusho - kee-oo-shoh pressure points
Ukemi - *ooh-kem-ee* safety procedures; the art of falling correctly, so as to not obtain severe injury
Tobi - *toh-bee* jumping (i.e. Mae Tobi Geri - jumping front kick)
Empi - *ehm-pee* elbow (i.e. Empi Uchi - elbow strike)
Hiza - *hih-zah* knee (i.e. Hiza Geri - knee kick)
Te - *tay* hand
Hazushi - *hah-zoo-shih* to release (i.e. Hazushi-Te - to release hand)
Niguru - *nih-ghu-rooh* yielding (i.e. Kakato Niguru - single hand grab yielding method)

Numbers

Ichi - *ee-chee* one 1
Ni - *nee* two 2
San - *sahn* three 3
Shi - *she* four 4
  Yon - *yhon* four/fourth 4 or 4th
Go - *goh* five 5
Roku - *roh-koo* six 6
Shichi - *shih-chee* seven 7
  Nana - *nah-nah* seven/seventh (Okinawan origin) 7 or 7th
Hachi - *ha-chee* eight 8
Ku - *kooh* nine 9
Ju - *jew* ten 10

Black Belt Ranks

Shodan - *sho-dohn* 1st Degree Black Belt
Nidan - *nee-dohn* 2nd Degree Black Belt
Sandan - *sahn-dohn* 3rd Degree Black Belt
Yondan - *yhon-dohn* 4th Degree Black Belt
Godan - *goh-dohn* 5th Degree Black belt
Rokudan - *roh-koo-dohn* 6th Degree Black Belt
Shichidan - *she-chee-dohn* 7th Degree Black Belt
Hachidan - *hah-chee-dohn* 8th Degree Black Belt
Kudan - *kooh-dohn* 9th Degree Black Belt

Judan - *jew-dohn* 10th Degree Black Belt

Titles

Sempai - *sem-pie* senior student
Shidoshi - *she-doh-she* an instructor (basic level)
Sensei - *sen-say* a teacher
Fuku-Shihan – *foo-koo she-hon* assistant instructor (assistant to the chief instructor)
Renshi - *rhen-she* a polished instructor
Shihan - *she-hon* chief instructor; model teacher
Kyoshi - *kee-oh-she* senior instructor
Hanshi - *hon-she* grand master
Soke - *soh-kay* an inheritor of a system of martial arts
Soke Dai - *soh-kay-diee* an inheritor of a system of martial arts ranking 8th Dan or higher
Sho Dai Soke - *sho-diee-soh-kay* the first generation grand master (founder) of a system of martial arts
Ni Dai Soke - *nee-diee-soh-kay* the second-generation grand aster of a system of martial arts (usually the first heir to Sho Dai Soke)

Standard Ranking System

10th Kyu – *Jukyu* White Belt
9th Kyu – *Kukyu* White Belt
8th Kyu – *Hachikyu* White Belt
7th Kyu – *Shichikyu* Yellow Belt
6th Kyu – *Rokukyu* Yellow Belt
5th Kyu – *Gokyu* Blue Belt
4th Kyu – *Yonkyu* Green Belt
3rd Kyu – *Sankyu* Brown Belt
2nd Kyu – *Nikyu* Brown Belt
1st Kyu – *Ikkyu* Brown Belt
1st Dan – *Shodan* 1st Degree Black Belt
2nd Dan – *Nidan* 2nd Degree Black Belt
3rd Dan – *Sandan* 3rd Degree Black Belt
4th Dan – *Yondan* 4th Degree Black Belt
5th Dan – *Godan* 5th Degree Black Belt
6th Dan – *Rokudan* 6th Degree Black Belt
7th Dan – *Shichidan* 7th Degree Black Belt
8th Dan – *Hachidan* 8th Degree Red Belt

9th Dan – *Kudan* 9th Degree Red Belt
10th Dan – *Judan* 10th Degree Red Belt

Grading

Black Belt – Please note that the pace of Black Belt advancement for those who complete ***Mokuroku*** training and certification is placed at the Senior Shihan's (Dai Shihan) discretion.

NOTE: all rank certificates are issued by the International Combat Aiki-jujutsu Federation, and bear the signature and seal of the Kaicho.

NOTES

NOTES

NOTES

NOTES

NOTES

NOTES

NOTES

Ranking System

Belt Color	Kyu/Dan Grade
White	10th Kyu White Belt
Yellow	8th Kyu Yellow Belt
Blue	6th Kyu Blue Belt
Green	4th Kyu Green Belt
3rd Brown	3rd Kyu Brown Belt
2nd Brown	2nd Kyu Brown Belt
1st Brown	1st Kyu Brown Belt
1st Degree Black Belt	Shodan - 1st Degree Black Belt
2nd Degree Black Belt	Nidan - 2nd Degree Black Belt
3rd Degree Black Belt	Sandan - 3rd Degree Black Belt
4th Degree Black Belt	Yondan - 4th Degree Black Belt
5th Degree Black Belt	Godan - 5th Degree Black Belt
6th Degree Black Belt	Rokudan - 6th Degree Black Belt
7th Degree Black Belt	Shichidan - 7th Degree Black Belt
8th Degree Black Belt	Hachidan - 8th Degree Black Belt (Kyoshi)
9th Degree Black Belt	Honorary Kudan - 9th Degree Red Belt (Hanshi)
10th Degree Black Belt	Honorary Judan - 10th Degree Red Belt (Hanshi)

ICAJF INTRODUCTION

The International Combat Aiki-jujutsu Federation (ICAJF) welcomes all practitioners of Aiki arts into the fraternal fellowship and community of our organization. ICAJF recognizes, endorses and promotes the principles, techniques and philosophies of combat arts stemming from Japan.

We offer our members the following:

- ***Annual Affiliate Membership***
- ***Full Lifetime Membership***
- ***Internationally Recognized and Certified Rank***
- ***Internationally Recognized and Certified Instructor Certification***
- ***Style/System Recognition and Endorsement***
- ***Headmaster/Kaiso Certification***

The International Combat Aiki-jujutsu Federation is an international fellowship of Aiki practitioners. This is the open-art branch of Nihon Goshin Daito-ryu Aiki-jujutsu Renmei.

LEGAL STATUS

The International Combat Aiki-jujutsu Federation is a branch of the Sentou-ryu Aikikai, which is a non-profit organization incorporated in the Commonwealth of Kentucky. Sentou-ryu Aikikai is currently establishing its tax-exempt status as an educational/sports fraternal organization.

PURPOSE

The International Combat Aiki-jujutsu Federation is organized specifically for the following purposes:

1. To provide a means of training in Aiki-based arts
2. To preserve the knowledge and integrity of Aiki-based systems, including Aiki-jujutsu/Aikido/Jujutsu and its various derivatives
3. To provide a means of fellowship amongst various branches of Aiki-based organizations

4. To provide an avenue of recognition for practitioners of Aiki-based systems
5. To establish basic guidelines by which all members will observe
6. To provide a means of certification and validation for practitioners of Aiki-based arts
7. To recognize, certify and endorse member schools (dojos), clubs and study groups
8. To recognize, sanction and endorse new and unique systems based on the principles and philosophies of Aiki-based arts

MISSION STATEMENT

The mission of the International Combat Aiki-jujutsu Federation is to provide an atmosphere of fellowship and brotherhood among all practitioners of Aiki-based arts; to promote, endorse, teach and convey the principles, philosophies and techniques of Aiki-based arts; to continue and preserve the traditional aspects, both in concept and application of Aiki-jujutsu/Aikido/Jujutsu; to provide our members with valid and recognized certification; and to promote an arena by which all members may expand their technical skills and abilities.

ICAJF KAMON

The official Kamon (emblem/logo) of the International Combat Aiki-jujutsu Federation is a voided (black and white) flower. The full-color version is awarded only to those who have studied, practiced and obtained ranking above Godan (5th Degree Black Belt) issued by ICAJF. The black and white version is the general symbol used by all members of ICAJF.

The Kamon is a registered and trademarked emblem, protected by copyright.

MEMBERSHIP

Membership in the International Combat Aiki-jujutsu Federation is open to all who seek to practice, train and preserve the traditional Japanese Aiki-based arts. ICAJF offers levels of membership, which serves as a support mechanism for the established purposes of the International Combat Aiki-jujutsu Federation.

All members are required to adhere to the rules and regulations of the International Combat Aiki-jujutsu Federation at all times. The rules of this Federation are contained within this publication, and serve as general guidelines for the purpose of promoting our efforts.

Membership in the International Combat Aiki-jujutsu Federation is granted on a lifetime basis. We do not seek to charge exorbitant fees, collect annual dues, etc. We seek only to promote and endorse the fundamental aspects, which are the basis of all Aiki-based arts.

The traditional Code will be observed by all members at all times. This code is referred to as the, "Code of Bushido," or the, "Bushido Code," also known as the, "Samurai Code," which is as follows:

The Samurai Bushido Code (Japanese "way of the warrior", or bushido), was the warrior code of the samurai.

Samurai Warrior Code was a strict code that demanded:

- loyalty
- devotion
- and honor to the death

Under this code, if a samurai warrior failed to uphold his honor he could regain it by performing seppuku (ritual suicide).

The samurai bushido code is an internally-consistent ethical code, grounded in the spiritual approach of the Rinzai school of Zen Buddhism.

In its purest form, it demands of its practitioners that they look effectively backward at the present from the moment of their own death, as if they were already, in effect, dead.

The Bushido of the Samurai was also a spiritual basis for those who committed kamikaze attacks during World War II.

For this reason many of the martial arts that are rooted in Japanese Bushido were banned by the occupying Americans during the post-war occupation.

Bushido is still practiced today (in modified forms) and in many of today's modern martial arts. The most common forms of bushido martial arts, still practiced in Japan today, are:

- judo
- karate
- jujutsu
- aikido
- kendo

The modern sport of kendo takes its basic philosophy from Japanese Bushido, in particular, the theory that the entire purpose of the sport is "one cut, one kill".

Unlike in other martial arts, extended contact, or multiple strikes, tends to be discouraged in favor of clean single strokes on the body or the head.

There are **seven virtues associated with the samurai bushido code**:

- **Gi** - Rectitude
- **Yu** - Courage
- **Jin** - Benevolence
- **Rei** - Respect
- **Makoto** - Honesty
- **Meiyo** - Honor
- **Chugi** - Loyalty

Re: *http://www.bigbearacademy.com/bushido-code.html*

MEMBERSHIP FEES

Affiliate Membership: $35.00 per year
Affiliate Membership is open to any individual, despite race, creed, color, national origin, physical handicap, or martial arts discipline. Affiliate Membership dues are $35.00 per year. However, under this type of membership, the member is not afforded the opportunity to gain Rank Recognition, Rank Certification/Advancement, Instructor Certification/Titles, and/or Dojo Charters. The member will be listed on the ICAJF web site as a member in good standing. However, the listing will contain only the member's name and country. No indication of rank, style/system or Instructor status will be listed. This type of membership is granted a membership certificate and membership card printed on card stock, which must be renewed annually.

Associate Membership: $100.00
Associate Membership is open to any individual, despite race, creed, color, national origin, physical handicap, or martial arts discipline. Associate Membership dues are $100.00 (1st year) and $50.00 per year annual renewal. However, under this type of membership, the member is not afforded the opportunity to gain Rank Certification/Advancement, Instructor Certification/Titles, and/or Dojo Charters. The member will be listed on the ICAJF web site as a member in good standing. However, the listing will contain only the member's name and country. No indication of rank, style/system or Instructor status will be listed. This type of membership is granted a membership certificate and membership card printed on card stock and a Rank Recognition certificate, which must be renewed annually.

Full Lifetime Membership: $250.00
Full Lifetime Membership is open to any individual, despite race, creed, color, national origin, physical handicap, or martial arts discipline. Full Lifetime Membership dues are $250.00. This type of membership is granted the opportunity to gain Rank Recognition, Rank Certification/Advancement, Instructor Certification/Titles, and/or Dojo Charters. The member will be listed on the ICAJF web site as a member in good standing. However, the listing will contain only the member's name, rank, style/system and country. This type of membership is granted for a lifetime.

Lifetime Dojo Charter Membership: $250.00
Dojo Membership is granted to those individuals who desire to be recognized for their accomplishment in achieving Black Belt status and are active in conveying the arts. This type of membership is open to any individual, despite race, creed, color, national origin, physical handicap, or martial arts discipline. However, the member must provide adequate proof of Black Belt status by means of submitting a photocopy of his/her current Dan (Black Belt) grading certificate. ICAJF will accept only certifications that are issued by the member's Sensei, or through the Hombu (Headquarters) of the member's particular style/system. The member must also provide proof of owning/operating a martial arts school, club or study group. This type of membership is afforded the following:

- 10 Student Membership Cards per year
- 10 Uniform Patches per year
- Dojo Charter Certificate

Dojo Members (Chief Instructor) are afforded the opportunity to gain Rank Recognition, Rank Certification/Advancement, Instructor Certification/Titles, and/or Style/system recognition (Headmaster & Sokeship Council). The member will be listed on the ICAJF web site as a member in good standing. The listing will contain the member's name, rank, style/system and country. The school, club or study group will also be listed on the web site with a link to the school, club or study group's web site and contact information. This type of membership is granted a membership certificate and card printed on card stock, which must be renewed annually. Annual renewal for Dojo Charter Membership is $100.00.

RANK RECOGNITION

The International Combat Aiki-jujutsu Federation will provide suitable rank recognition certificates to those who qualify. In order to qualify for rank recognition, the member must provide adequate proof of rank/qualification. The member will submit his/her current rank certificate, issued by the member's Sensei, or through the Hombu (Headquarters) of the member's particular style/system. Once this has been verified by the Grading Board, the member will be issued an official ICAJF Rank Recognition certificate, bearing the member's current rank.

ICAJF provides rank recognition certificates on 11" x 17" card stock, bearing the logos, seals and hanko (seal) of the Federation and the signature of the Headmaster.

RANK CERTIFICATION

The International Combat Aiki-jujutsu Federation will validate and certify ranks in Aiki-jujutsu, Combat Aikido or Jujutsu. Rank Certification fees are reasonable. The certification process is as follows:

ICAJF Dan Certification and Teaching Titles are based on technical ability, teaching ability, and character development. In the case of Dan grades, more emphasis is placed on technical ability. Teaching Titles, which are more difficult to achieve, place more emphasis on personal development and teaching ability.

NOTE: Teaching titles allow instructors to recommend individuals to the ICAJF for ranks two levels below their own.

The support one has given the ICAJF, the recommendations of one's seniors in the ICAJF, and the contributions that one has made to the martial arts, are major considerations for promotion. ICAJF time-in-grade requirements for promotion apply to all members of ICAJF. In cases of uniquely talented individuals and/or professional instructors, an altered schedule of promotion may be approved by the officials of ICAJF. Time-in-grade requirements for Renshi, Shihan, Kyoshi and Hanshi can be waived for qualified instructors when they initially join the ICAJF.

All applicants for rank/title are thoroughly examined by the ICAJF Directors. Rank issued by mainstream, well-known Japanese associations will frequently by recognized by the ICAJF. Ranking from lesser-known groups, will delay certification and may possibly require an in-person examination conducted by appropriate ICAJF officials.

Members may acquire advance rank and training by one of the following methods:

Nihon Goshin Daito-ryu Aikijujutsu:

- The member must be in good standing with the International Combat Aiki-jujutsu Federation
- The member must hold a Black Belt in some system/style of martial arts
- The member must attend and participate in a total of 4 monthly cross training/ranking camps
- Upon completion of the 4 monthly training camps, the member will test for Black Belt in Daito-ryu Aiki-bujutsu
- If approved, the member will be certified as a Black Belt with the rank of Shodan in Nihon Goshin Daito-ryu Aikijujutsu with a valid and verify able lineage

Aiki-jujutsu/Jujutsu/Aikibudo:
Kyu/Dan Grades

- The member must be in good standing with the International Combat Aiki-jujutsu Federation
- The member must attend and participate in Grading Exam before the Grading Board
- The member will demonstrate the basic techniques, including throws, joint-locks, take-downs and arresting techniques
- The member will demonstrate the weapons disarming techniques, including knife, club, stick and gun (Brown & Black Belt level)

If approved by the Grading Board, the member will be certified with appropriate rank

Rank Advancement:
Dan Grades

- All member Black Belts holding the rank of Rokudan or above may request advancement in rank to the next highest Dan grade without examination in conjunction with time-in-grade and age requirements.
- All members must ensure that they have satisfied the minimum time-in-grade requirements before making request

- For members ranking below Rokudan, an examination will be required. Upon approval of the Headmaster of International Combat Aiki-jujutsu Federation, the member may submit thru requirements for his/her rank advancement exam via video, or in-person during a regularly scheduled advancement examination, which will be held before the Examining Board

PLEASE NOTE
+ALL RANK CERTIFICATIONS MUST BE EARNED VIA EXAM+

RANK CERTIFICATION FEES

Rank Promotion/Certification Fees:

8th - 3rd Kyu: $25.00 per exam
2nd - 1st Kyu: $60.00 per exam
Shodan (1st Degree Black Belt): ***$100.00***
Nidan (2nd Degree Black Belt): ***$150.00***
Sandan (3rd Degree Black Belt): ***$200.00***
Yondan (4th Degree Black Belt): ***$250.00***
Godan (5th Degree Black Belt): ***$300.00***
Rokudan (6th Degree Black Belt): ***$350.00***
Shichidan (7th Degree Black Belt) ***$400.00***
Hachidan (8th Degree Black Belt): ***$450.00***
Kudan (9th Degree Black Belt): ***Bestowed as Honorary Rank***
Judan (10th Degree Black Belt): ***Bestowed as Honorary Rank***

CERTIFICATION EXAMINATIONS

Kyu/Dan Grades:
The Grading Board of the International Combat Aiki-jujutsu Federation will convene twice per year in June and November to provide opportunity for rank certification examinations. The examination will consist of, but is not limited to the following:

- Ukemi Waza
- Atemi Waza
- Aiki no Waza

- Juho no Waza
- Nage no Waza
- Katame no Waza
- Goshin Waza

The Grading Board will request standard and advanced techniques based upon rank and level. The Uke of the candidate will be provided by the Grading Board. The candidate will also provide the following:

- The Candidate's training background
- The Candidate's teaching background (if any)
- The Candidate's current grading certificate (copy)
- Letter of recommendation by the Candidate's Sensei, or a Senior member of the Grading Board

Instructor Certification Examination:
The Grading Board of the International Combat Aiki-jujutsu Federation will convene twice per year in June and November to provide opportunity for instructor certification examinations. The examination will consist of, but is not limited to the following:

- First Aid Certification
- CPR Certification
- History of Aiki-jujutsu
- Knowledge of the grading system (both Kyu/Dan and Menkyo system)
- Written documentation of logged training/instruction hours

The above examination will be required for any individual to gain Teaching License (Title).

TIME-IN-GRADE REQUIREMENTS

Minimum Age/Time-In-Grade Requirements:

Rank:	Minimum Age:	Minimum Time-in-grade:
Shodan-Ho	***16***	-------
Shodan	**18**	-------
Nidan	***19***	1 year after Shodan
Sandan	***21***	2 years after Nidan
Yondan	***24***	3 years after Sandan
Godan	***28***	4 years after Yondan
Rokudan	***33***	5 years after Godan
Shichidan	***39***	6 years after Rokudan
Hachidan	***46***	7 years after Shichidan
Kudan	***54***	8 years after Hachidan
Judan	***63***	9 years after Kudan

HOMOLOGATION

Homologation: The issuance of rank certificate in a closely related art equal to current rank. This is done only occasionally where a legitimate reason for the cross ranking is demonstrated.

In order for a member to receive cross-ranking, the member must provide his/her training syllabus, which should be detailed and outlines as follows:

To earn my Yellow Belt, I had to learn the following:

1. Front fall
2. Side fall (right/left sides)
3. Forward roll
4. Backward roll
5. Gedan barai
6. Jodan Uke
7. Chudan Uke

To earn my Orange Belt, I had to learn the following:

1. Forward Diving roll
2. Jumping/Somersault roll

3. Grab releasing techniques (Hazushite)
    a) straight grab
    b) cross hand grab
    c) two-on-one hand grab
4. Major Hip Throw
5. Major Reaping Throw
6. ect.

INSTRUCTOR CERTIFICATION

Instructor Certification issued by the International Combat Aiki-jujutsu Federation requires the member to provide proof of the following:

- First Aid Certification (Adult/Child) by the American Red Cross or American Heart Association
- CPR Certification (Adult/Child) by the American Red Cross or American Heart Association

Once the member has received certification via the American Red Cross or American Heart Association, or some other valid certification bureau, the member will be granted his/her Instructor Certification.

> **NOTE**: Instructor Certification is only bestowed upon those members who are active in teaching and have obtained a Dojo Charter from the International Combat Aiki-jujutsu Federation. Chief Instructors of chartered Dojos may request that their teaching staff become certified through ICAJF. However, in order to do so, the Chief Instructor must submit a Letter of Recommendation on behalf of his/her assistant. The Assistant Instructor must be a recognized and registered Black Belt member of the International Combat Aiki-jujutsu Federation in good standing.

The International Combat Aiki-jujutsu Federation issues the following Instructor Certifications, upon satisfaction of the above requirements:

Instructor Certification: this is a "basic" instructor certification issued to 1st - 4th Dan

Master Instructor Certification: this is an "advanced" instructor certification issued to 5th Dan and higher

INSTRUCTOR LICENSURE

Instructor Certification Examination:

The Grading Board of the International Combat Aiki-jujutsu Federation will convene twice per year in June and November to provide opportunity for instructor certification examinations. The examination will consist of, but is not limited to the following:

- First Aid Certification (Adult/Child)
- CPR Certification (Adult/Child)
- History of Aiki-jujutsu
- Knowledge of the grading system (both Kyu/Dan and Menkyo system)
- Written documentation of logged training/instruction hours which must be documented by an Official in the member's Grading and License Passport issued by ICAJF

The above examination will be required for any individual to gain Teaching License (Title).

The International Combat Aiki-jujutsu Federation issues the following Instructor Licenses (Titles):

- **Fuku-Shidoin**: 1st - 3rd Dan
- **Shidoin**: 4th - 5th Dan
- **Renshi**: 5th dan and higher minimum of 1 year after advancement to 5th Dan
- **Shihan**: 6th Dan and higher minimum of 1 year after advancement to 6th Dan
- **Kyoshi**: 7th Dan and higher minimum of 2 years after advancement to 7th Dan
- **Hanshi**: 8th Dan and higher minimum of 2 years after advancement to 8th Dan

It is to be noted that the bestowal of titles is based upon longevity and contributions to the art - Titles are not based upon rank only.

Additionally, the member will be required to wait a minimum of one (1) to two (2) years at the noted minimal rank before consideration will be given for the bestowal of Instructor License and Title.

INSTRUCTOR CERTIFICATION/TITLE FEES

Fuku-Shidoin:	***$100.00***
Shidoin:	***$150.00***
Renshi:	***$200.00***
Shihan:	***$250.00***
Kyoshi:	***$300.00***
Hanshi:	***$350.00***

DOJO/CLUB CHARTERS

Dojos/Clubs/Study-groups who practice, teach and promote Aiki-jujutsu/Aiki-jutsu, Aikido, Jujutsu/Jujitsu are welcome to acquire official lifetime Dojo Charters from the International Combat Aiki-jujutsu Federation. Recognized and registered Dojos receive the following:

- Membership Certificate for Chief Instructor
- Rank Recognition Certificate for Chief Instructor
- Membership Card for Chief Instructor
- Instructor Certification for Chief Instructor
- 5 Student Membership Cards
- 5 Uniform Patches
- Dojo Charter Certificate

Chartered Dojos may register their students at the cost of $15.00 per student. In order to receive the ICAJF Kyu Grade member card the Dojo Cho will submit $15.00 per student along with the student's name and current rank.

Student membership cards are $25.00. The Instructor retains $10.00 and submits only $15.00 per student.

Please note that there is requirement of a minimum of five (5) student registrations per Dojo at a time.

Student Kyu-grade Certificates are available through the secured member area of our web site at a reduced rate.

STYLE/SYSTEM RECOGNITION

The International Combat Aiki-jujutsu Federation recognizes, endorses and sanctions systems of Aiki-jujutsu (and its derivatives). The Headmaster/Founder of each system is required to meet stringent qualifications before induction into the ICAJF Headmaster & Kaiso Council. Opportunity for new systems to gain recognition is provided in a fair, non-political manner.

The requirements are as follows:

1. The Headmaster/Founder must provide sufficient proof that he/she is either the legitimate heir or founder of the system.
2. The Headmaster/Founder will supply adequate proof of the following:

    A) A minimum of a 5th Degree Black Belt in a recognized and sanctioned system of Aiki-jujutsu, Aikido, Aiki-budo, or Jujutsu

    B) A minimum of at least two (2) other Dan grades in two other sanctioned and recognized systems/styles of martial arts

    C) A minimum of at least one (1) teaching certification (Master Level)

    D) Submission of the history and philosophy of the system to be sanctioned

    NOTE: the style/system must be "unique" and "original"

    E) Submission of the training/grading history of the Headmaster/Founder including dates, instructors and contact information

F) Submission of the Training/Grading Syllabus of the new system up to and including 3rd Degree Black Belt

3. The candidate will supply a minimum of three (3) Letters of Recommendation from martial artists who are familiar with the candidate and his/her system.
   NOTE: Letters of Recommendation can not and will not be accepted from members who are related to the candidate by either blood or marriage.
4. The candidate will submit a video (DVD) of him/herself performing the required techniques of the new system up to and including 3rd Degree Black Belt.

Upon review by the members of the International Combat Aiki-jujutsu Federation Headmaster and Kaiso Council, the candidate will be notified of the findings of the Council and if favorable, the candidate will be received into the Headmaster and Kaiso Council.

New systems/styles recognized by International Combat Aiki-Jujutsu Federation will receive a Letter of Recognition (Proclamation of Recognition) of the new system/style, which will be signed and sealed by all members of the Headmaster and Kaiso Council. Additionally, the Headmaster/Founder of the recognized and sanctioned style/system will be granted rank in accordance to age and ability.

> **NOTE**: The International Combat Aiki-Jujutsu Federation **will not** issue and/or bestow ranks of 8th - 10th Dan upon any individual who does not meet the minimum age requirements.

HEADMASTER & KAISO COUNCIL

The Headmaster and Kaiso Council of the International Combat Aiki-jujutsu Federation is comprised of Headmasters, Head of Family, Kaiso (Founders), Nidai Soke/Soke (Inheritors) who can validate their system according to the requirements for Style/System recognition and/or provide adequate proof that the member is the bona-fied inheritor of the style/system presented.

It should be noted that Kaiso will be granted recognition as such. However, since they are the Head Founder of their own system, they fall out of the usual Dan grades and will therefore not be presented with Rank Certification, unless he/she can provide the required proof of current grade and rank, as well as the additional Dan rankings required for Style/System recognition. In this case, the member will be granted only the highest Dan grade for his/her particular age and time-in-grade.

For those members of the International Combat Aiki-jujutsu Federation that qualify for induction into the Headmaster and Kaiso Council, ICAJF will issue the following:

- Lifetime Membership Certificate Headmaster/Kaiso Council
- Lifetime Member Identification Card
- Rank Certification Menjo (11" x 17")
- Instructor/Title Certification (11" x 17")
- Lifetime Dojo Charter
- System/Style recognition letter, signed by the Headmaster of ICAJF
- ICAJF Headmaster/Kaiso Council Certificate printed on 11" x 17" quality card stock, bearing the seals, logos and signature of ICAJF and the Headmaster of ICAJF

The International Combat Aiki-jujutsu Federation requires that any individual who is seeking Style/System recognition and induction into the Headmaster and Kaiso Council to pay a one-time fee in the amount of $500.00.

INTERNATIONAL COMBAT AIKI-JUJUTSU FEDERATION
P. O. Box 11763
Louisville, KY 40251 USA
www.icajf.com

www.ingramcontent.com/pod-product-compliance
Ingram Content Group UK Ltd.
Pitfield, Milton Keynes, MK11 3LW, UK
UKHW020229250726
13967UKWH00001B/268

9 780557 715381